Mike Powell
A GAME TO LOVE

In Celebration of Tennis

Edited by Lewis Blackwell

Abrams, New York

in association with PQ Blackwell

Tennis has gi

ven me soul.

Martina Navratilova

Serena is all strength,
a more compact shape,
while Venus is all legs
and arms and plays
very well with that.

Warm-up

I think the first tennis match that I photographed professionally was John McEnroe versus Björn Borg at Wimbledon in 1981. It turned out to be one of the great finals. This was the year Borg finally lost his crown, and this was the last match he played at Wimbledon; the beginning of the end of his career. McEnroe won 4–6, 7–6, 7–6, 6–4, and in doing so confirmed himself at the top of the sport. It was back when you could still line up to get into the Wimbledon final as there was a free-standing public area. I had just started at the agency Allsport Photography, run by my brother Steve and Tony Duffy. I had become a member of the National Union of Journalists in Britain to get an NUJ press card and one from AIPS (Association Internationale de la Presse Sportive)—the sports journalist credentials I needed to attend other events around Europe. There was a line of fans who had been waiting through the night, but with my press card I could simply walk into the grounds five minutes before they opened up to the public. So as a cub reporter, age sixteen, I strolled in with my not-very-impressive camera and lenses and took my pick of the positions in the free-standing area. I don't remember taking any great pictures that day, but my enthusiasm was whetted. It was enough for me then just to be there. If nothing else, there began my love affair with press passes.

I love shooting athletes of all kinds, and the events they take part in. Tennis players and the tournaments have particular qualities

The champions, the players who really go all the way, have this incredible ability to focus so that they play every point as if it is the most important thing.

and traditions. I shot tennis at the start of my career, mainly in the US, and this was a bedrock of my own development as a photographer. I was shooting Andre Agassi when he had hair and wore acid-wash denim shorts. The tennis players of that period were treated like rock stars by the newspapers in the UK; what some of them did was front page news, jumping well outside of the sports section. There were big characters who seemed to mean a lot to the public, and this helped the game get huge. Indeed, tennis was perhaps a key sport that encouraged the media to look at the participants as more than just athletes, seeing in their performance, on and off the court, the potential to build celebrities and create really human stories for the fans to follow.

Infinite Loop

What is distinctive about shooting tennis and following the tour is that you get to do a great deal of it. There is tennis happening throughout the day, all aspects of it, with many different matches within a tournament and often several going on simultaneously. You get to shoot in all kinds of light, which is something I really enjoy about tennis. You can work from early to late, during the evening, and into the night under floodlights. During a Grand Slam there is always something going on, and you are shooting as the conditions

change. Photography is about light, first and foremost, and with tennis you get to really explore how light interacts with the athletes and the play. The basic elements of the court may not seem to change much—the players, lines, net, and so on—and the range of movements might be thought of as quite repetitive. But different courts have different light at different times, with various angles and backgrounds, and all that is before the incredible variety of players step out there, each with subtly unique ways of doing things, and probably a determination to do something special that day. You are constantly able to explore this shifting light, which means every match has the potential to deliver something remarkable in terms of an image. You learn where the light is likely to be and how it will change over time, all of which influences where you are going to be. Compare this with, say, a football game, which starts at night and ends at night and the light doesn't change much. The potential of how images can look is that much more restricted, whereas in a tennis tournament you have greater range to work with. In a Grand Slam such as the US Open you might start in the middle of the morning and end up going on until the early hours—that is an incredible range of lighting situations to explore, with constant action to focus on and each match bringing new variables to respond to.

For me, the lighting range of a great tennis tournament is matched by only a few other sports. You can get great variety at some of the epic motor sport events that go on around the world, like the Baja 1000, where you start predawn and end the next day as you follow the rally, or the Le Mans 24-hour race. At the Olympic Games you can be shooting three or four events throughout the day in different environments with changing light. But it is remarkable that I have to make these comparisons; to do this against one sport with an apparently narrow range of activity that takes place on the seemingly rigid setting of a tennis court. This game, more than any other, I think, gives you that opportunity to really focus on working with light, the discipline that is at the heart of great photography. At one o'clock in the afternoon you are working with short shadows; everything looks hard in the overhead light. In the late evening, everything is bathed with that beautiful light that gives a glow and a warmth to the image. And in between, and depending on the weather, you have an almost infinite range of conditions to work with. All that variety can be happening on the same court, with the same basic elements transformed through light.

A downside of the wonderful riches of a great tennis tournament is that sometimes there is too much going on—you just can't shoot it all. So you have to be quite analytical and plan the work intelligently: you think who is playing whom on the court, what time of day it is, what the weather is doing, and more. This dictates your working process and will frame what photographs you might produce that day. It can be stressful, but it is also exciting—you have these ever-changing environments and related conditions that keep offering you the potential to do something fresh.

The Human Factor

The wonder of light in tennis is something a photographer can get excited about but, of course, what we all connect with is that there is a fantastic human contest to document. If it is a good game, if the players are really reacting and expressing emotion, if the crowd is really into it, then all this rubs off on me...undoubtedly the adrenalin gets through into the kind of pictures you make. It opens up many more visual possibilities if you have interesting things happening with the crowd: the spectators react to the action, the players react to the crowd and respond after each point, and, as the tension becomes that much more highly strung, there is potential for exciting things to photograph. The athletic feats, the great lunges and leaps get that much more astounding. The great play and

Rafael Nadal is particularly notable for playing every point like it is match point—which is perhaps how you get to be number one, and also how you get super-fit and test your body to the brink of destruction.

As it always comes down to playing just a few points better in these epic matches, that mental edge is the difference between being one of the great champions and being just a very good player.

the great action shots tend to come in those games that are the hardest, where players are really being tested. Where the crowd is a cauldron of excitement, full of noise and expectation, that's when there is an opportunity for capturing some remarkable energy in the image. But there is also a lot to be said for the quieter moments: perhaps a late evening on an outside court, with people just enjoying watching the tennis, and the energy is on the court with a more serene scene surrounding. In that situation you may get to bring out more of the simple pleasure of playing or watching the game—and that, at root, is where it all begins. The fact is that whatever match it is, at a Grand Slam the players are competing for their professional careers; it's a little bit life-and-death. They want the ranking points; they always need to

win. At these major competitions, to progress one round is a notable step—or not—in the player's career. That applies to the stars as well as the players ranked in the hundreds: you either have a lot to win, or a lot to lose. The result of every match has consequences, in a way that doesn't really apply in many other sports, where your standing may be measured and averaged over a broader range of performance. The four Grand Slams in tennis have a weighting that can be very significant to the ranking and perception of a player.

Mind Games

The champions, the players who really go all the way, have this incredible ability to focus so that they play every point as if it is the most important thing. You don't see them give up on points; they chase every one down. It means they can get through early matches quickly, and that they are ready, with practiced intensity, for when the tougher challenges come in the later rounds. On the very odd occasion, when for some reason you note that a major player doesn't have that attitude together for the tournament, it is actually no surprise when they go out to a supposedly shocking defeat. Rafael Nadal is particularly notable for playing every point like it is match point—which is perhaps how you get to be number one, and also how you get super-fit and test your body to the brink of destruction. He just never lets up. It was particularly apparent when he met Novak Djokovic in the final at Flushing Meadows this year: they both had an incredible aura of intensity that day, but Rafa's was just that bit more, and unwaveringly consistent. As it always comes down to playing just a few points better in these epic matches, that mental edge is the difference between being one of the great champions and being just a very good player. And, for me as a photographer, watching and analyzing and responding throughout the match, somehow those mind games become palpable; they are something that I start to find apparent in the images that emerge during the match. I remember at 4–4 in the second set, when the rain came and interrupted play, we were

at an absolute key point. The excitement was immense, and I was really jacked up. These are the times you wait for, when you can get the hair standing up on your neck. But the rain came, there was a break, and then it took a few games before that energy started to build again. Even then, though, the different mood can give you other images, more reflective moments.

Life Through the Lens

As a photographer you actually don't get to see the match played in the way that a spectator does. You are focusing on a particular end, on a particular player, perhaps waiting for a particular action to happen... You spend a lot of time looking through the viewfinder of a camera. You are shooting for the moment and at the same time you are working across time. You are anticipating where the reaction is going to come from based on how important the point is, and to whom. If it is a break point, you know that the outcome will lead to reactions, possibly notable ones at both ends. You have to make a call.

I am shooting for these emotive moments in the big matches. Typically during the first week of a tournament, I might be concentrating more on the beauty of the light, on getting across the character of the event.

The French player Gael Monfils is a good player…a fantastic player to photograph, a wonderfully expressive athlete.

The great play and the great action shots tend to come in those games that are the hardest, where players are really being tested.

In this sense, it is a bit like telling a story: you start by establishing where you are and get some good background in so that people can connect with what it is all about...and then later in the second week the action is really cranked up, the stories and concerns much more embedded in the viewer's mind, so that you can focus in on the detail of the play and the emotion of the players. This range is fantastically attractive for the photographer—you can be somewhat indulgent in the earlier matches, playing with the artistic value of the image, but later you switch to a high-adrenalin action-shooter mode, and you are absolutely fixed on nailing the key moments of the culminating action.

I do enjoy those early days of a tournament when I can allow myself to wander around and look for something very different. If it is Wimbledon, for instance, with the evening light on the grass and huge crowds milling alongside the outside courts, you have something very characterful; if it is the US Open, I might try to utilize the effect of the nighttime lights and get across the atmosphere of New York in the background. At Roland Garros in Paris you have a compact environment, which seems to bring both an intensity and a politeness to the crowd—and of course there is the different circumstance of working with clay courts, with the red-brown colors that keep changing as they dry out and are then raked and watered. Melbourne is different again, where you can be working in challenging temperatures, and then can enjoy fantastic evening light.

Anticipation

Photographing a tennis tournament is a little like fortune-telling: you need to make your own luck sometimes and think ahead as to what might happen. For example, with Nadal, I know he has a great forehand follow-through and I will need to be on a particular point on the court so that I have a chance to capture that moment when he whips the racquet over the top of his head while his feet are way off the ground. He will do that shot many times in the match but there is going to be the odd time when he is more explosive and further off the ground, which makes for a really outstanding shot. As a photographer you have to be fascinated by the potential of the body shape, of what looks best, of what can really communicate the action and the character of the game. Another great shot in tennis is Federer's backhand follow-through, which is huge. However, while he will play it a lot, the thing you need to get is when he is under maximum pressure and brings the shot off when he is way off the ground, getting up over the ball. In that split second he looks

Serena is very hard to read—going from aggressive screaming in one game to a sweet, angelic look in a way that is quite unpredictable.

like he is flying, with his arms completely outstretched, his chest sticking out, and his hair going up. It takes something special to push Federer that far.

So the key is to study the movement of an athlete. With a tennis player, I will break down their game into different moments, identifying the more signature elements of their game. This will guide me in knowing what I might get from them and how I set myself up to photograph the match. I will be thinking of what movement looks the most graceful or the most powerful, and which movement best expresses the kind of game they play. Alongside this you are always expecting the unexpected—if that doesn't sound too crazy. And then there are times when you are shooting players you don't know and it will take you a few games to figure them out.

There is also the conundrum of how some players who might be very good are actually not that interesting to shoot while others, who may not be able to sustain a high ranking, have a certain something that really makes them good to photograph. The French player Gael Monfils is a good player, but never quite gets to the heights—and yet is a fantastic player to photograph, a wonderfully expressive athlete. I wish he would win more.

And no doubt he wishes that, too! He's a gold mine for photographers; an old-school character in some ways, playing shots that are not really necessary but can look great.

There are a lot more power players in women's tennis than not so long ago, and that gives you something very different to work with. The Williams sisters have had a big say in that, but it is a mistake to think they are so alike. Serena is all strength, a more compact shape, while Venus is all legs and arms and plays very well with that—so visually you get very different shapes. Then there are the women who make a lot of noise on court. This annoys some people but for a photographer it makes for very unusual expressions and some interesting pictures.

Drawing and developing the characters of tennis is a big part of the fun. It is like being a caricaturist at times. You have Nadal, with a quirky eyebrow move that is more extreme than anything practiced by Sean Connery; with Federer, you seem to have somebody whose sweat glands have been removed. Once you latch on to noticing distinctions, you can start to work to pull them out visually. Federer rarely reacts at all unless he is in trouble…and we have been seeing a bit more of that lately. He keeps it internal and just unleashes it at the end. In contrast,

There's no draw in tennis. These lovely oppositions—the polite culture over the underlying violence—make for a bottled-up excitement that explodes out in various moments.

Andy Murray can be seen going into dark places through the match if he is under pressure; he can seem quite tortured out there. Serena is very hard to read—going from aggressive screaming in one game to a sweet, angelic look in a way that is quite unpredictable.

Indeed, all players are doing basically the same thing—it's called tennis. But they each do it in their own way, and each draws unique sets of fans and a unique atmosphere around their games. All that gives tennis this infinite variety.

A Sense of Place

Having a fresh look at the Grand Slams after some years away has enabled me to see the differences between the four tournaments. I realized that the clichés that we all come to expect from the four cities do exist. Just take the ball boys and girls, for example. At Wimbledon they are really well turned out, always in the right place, perhaps a bit terrified of doing the wrong thing. In contrast, in New York they are more ragged, laughing and joking on court, which would never happen in Wimbledon. They throw the balls around in quite a casual way at Flushing Meadows. In Paris, they all seem to come from the same academy; they are drilled every morning, and are really fast across the court and agile. There is the polite silence around the court in Wimbledon but in New York you can be down in the photographer's pit during a night game and you can't hear yourself think for all the noise around. Even the photographers are on the telephone during the game, chitchatting. Part of winning a Grand Slam is dealing with all this—and to win in each place shows that you have the ability and the temperament to triumph on different kinds of courts and with a really different ambience.

Changing Cameras

The way we take photographs today with digital technology makes it very easy to get

We wanted to examine how tennis has such an amazing mix of the gladiatorial and the elegant, a fashion show in which the models are out to kill each other, in terms of the play.

There are moments inside of a tennis stroke that happen so fast that you only get to appreciate them when you see what they look like in an image.

shots that were hard in the past. The equipment allows you to get much closer, shoot at faster speeds, and have a high-quality image that freezes moments that you could never get with film. But shooting digital sets new challenges. You have to find a way to go further to stand out. One thing doesn't change: there is always room for the beautifully composed image that doesn't rely on technology but depends on your graphic eye.

The working conditions for a photographer have become much better. Where once we were just about tolerated at some locations,

now we are generally seen as a key part of communicating the wonder of the event and the sport. Melbourne and Paris are perhaps the places that treat photographers the best. The incredible access at Roland Garros over the years has meant there is a great heritage of showing the event. In New York it is more controlling and restricted, and even though Wimbledon has improved greatly, photographers' positions are still significantly fewer than you would get in Paris. But the lack of advertising signs and having an intimate crowd more than makes up for this. I love the dugouts at the end of the courts in Paris, where you can get to face some of the best serves in the world, literally shooting along the level of the court. We get to appreciate the clay of Paris in part because we can get so close to it. I was able to get on court at the end of Wimbledon and show just how worn the grass gets, but normally you can't really take that in.

Television is dominant in its positions, and leads how most of us can see the event, but the power of a great still image is that it will freeze a memory and make it iconic, in a way that the moving image doesn't. I like to study how players move and how they play their shots, but I can't break those down into thousandths of a second the way my camera can. There are moments inside of a tennis stroke that happen so fast that you only get to appreciate them when you see what they look like in an image. In these instances the photography becomes an investigation, an experiment to find out what is really going on. And it is not down to the motor drive—if you rely on that alone, you will miss the best things. Instead, you have to use your eye and imagination to anticipate when that play is going to happen and be ready with the fastest shutter speed to see what you can capture. You can go as high as perhaps one-eight-thousandth of a second in trying to pull one movement out that might exist in an explosive stroke. You might spend a lot of time trying to get something and keep ending up a tiny fraction of a second off, but when you get it, you are capturing an element that tells a story about why one player has performed so well.

Sweet Spot

I am fortunate in not being in competition with other tennis photographers—they are trying for something different when shooting for agencies or newspapers, while I have a much wider frame of reference. Of course, I am always keen to get the best version of the tournament-winning shot, but in general I am trying to do something more explorative than the pictures that appear in the newspapers. In this book we wanted to

get inside the spirit of the sport, to celebrate why in particular the four Grand Slam tournaments have emerged as something so emblematic of the game and of the countries where they are played.

And, most of all, we wanted to examine how tennis has such an amazing mix of the gladiatorial and the elegant, a fashion show in which the models are out to kill each other, in terms of the play. There's no draw in tennis. These lovely oppositions—the polite culture over the underlying violence—make for a bottled-up excitement that explodes out in various moments.

I am bearing my soul a bit in this book, putting out a lot of me through the images, trying to find whatever it is that excites me in tennis and in sport. What stands out are often details I noticed after being blind to them on previous occasions. The surprise in these shots comes out of that digging away at the action, looking to see it in a new fashion that wouldn't be seen that way even by somebody sitting next to you with the same camera and lenses. I had quite a few happy days on this book. And now, I hope you, the reader, will find your own moments of surprise and delight, and I am sure you won't need me to tell you when you hit that sweet spot.

Another great shot in tennis is Federer's backhand follow-through, which is huge. The thing you need to get is when he is under maximum pressure and brings the shot off when he is way off the ground, getting up over the ball. In that split second he looks like he is flying, with his arms completely outstretched, his chest sticking out and his hair going up. It takes something special to push Federer that far.

Grand Slams are electric, bursting with barely managed egos, tempers, and desires.

Monica Seles

Melbourne

It's a great place to start the year with reliable light helping the photographer's work and making many a gorgeous sunset. But for the players, they have to fear an extra opponent— the scorching heat that can evaporate talent and training if they don't hydrate correctly.

Mike Powell

courts 16-22

flushing meadows

wimbledon

margaret cou...

australian open
courts 4-15

australian open
sho...

roland garros

& 3

I call it the "Happy Slam." Roger Federer

Tennis is a perfect combination of violent action taking place in an atmosphere of total tranquility.

Billie Jean King

Women have certainly never hit harder and not just on account of improved equipment.
They're stronger, bigger, faster, better trained, and pushed above all by the example
of the Williams sisters. Serena, glorious and musclebound, and Venus, long-limbed and tall,
have redefined the sport around power. Michael Kimmelman

The only way of finding a solution is
to fight back, to move, to run, and to
control that pressure. Rafael Nadal

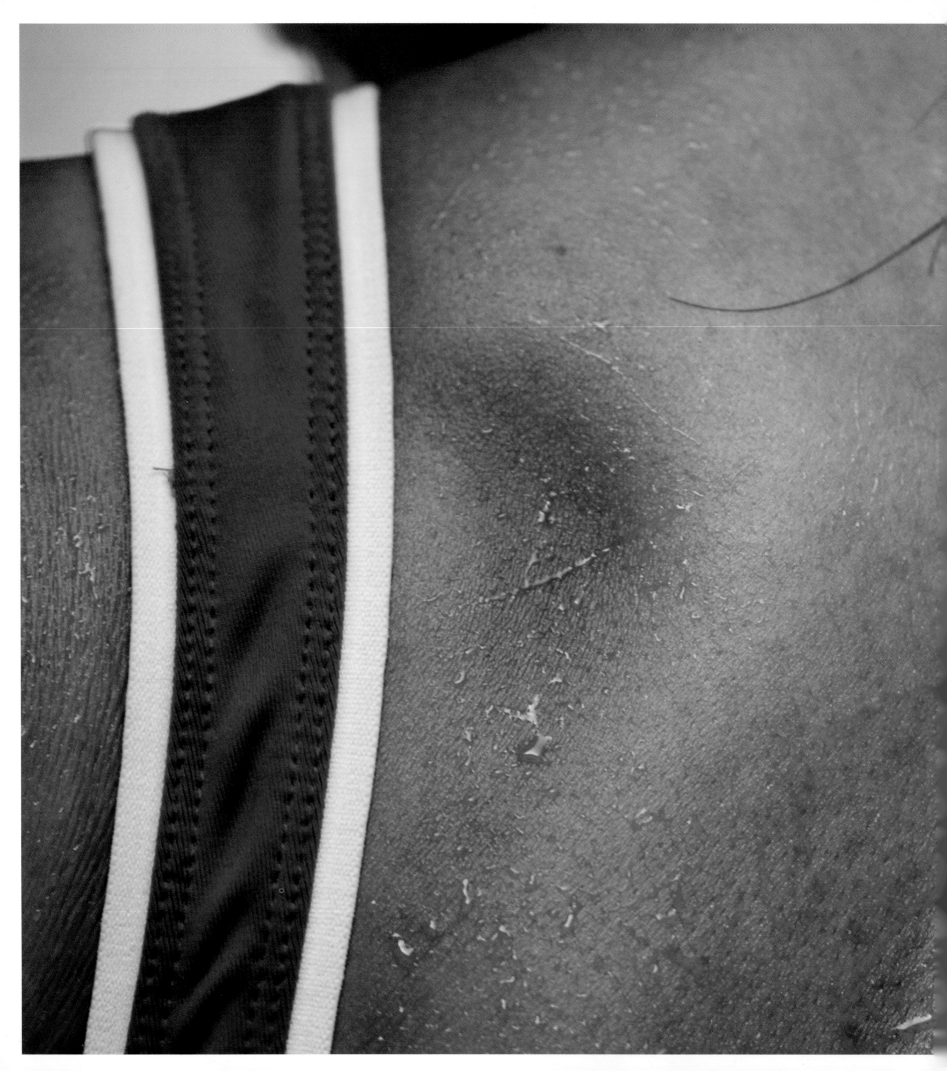

Champions keep playing until they get it right. Billie Jean King

I can cry like Roger; it's just a shame that
I can't play like him. Andy Murray

I always knew I had it in my hand. The question is:

do I have it in my mind and in my legs? Roger Federer

It's not enough to get close. The Williams girls were brought up by their parents not to feel good about losing. They were brought up to win. You give me the player who loves to win and hates to lose. That's a champion. John Wilkerson

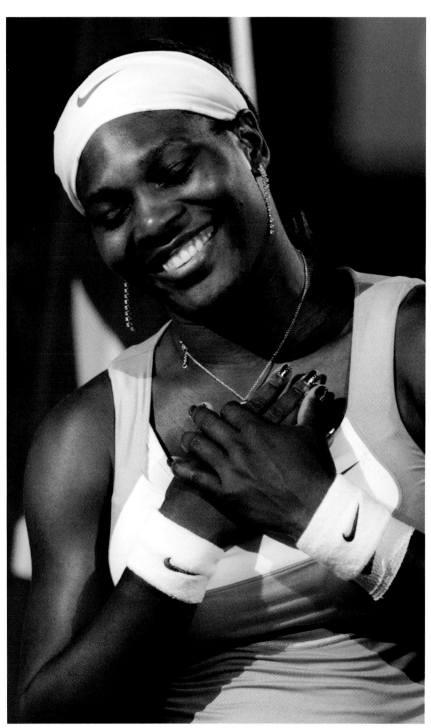

Paris

It's French, it's stylish, and you can get a nice steak for lunch with decent wine and good coffee. But out on the court, it's a dirty business, literally, as victories are ground out on the clay. Even the greatest champions need something different here.

Mike Powell

I'm French. We're in France. I hope they support me. Gael Monfils

Clay is the great equalizer; if you want to win here you'd better come with a strong mind, a big heart and a full repertoire of shots. Tim Ruffin

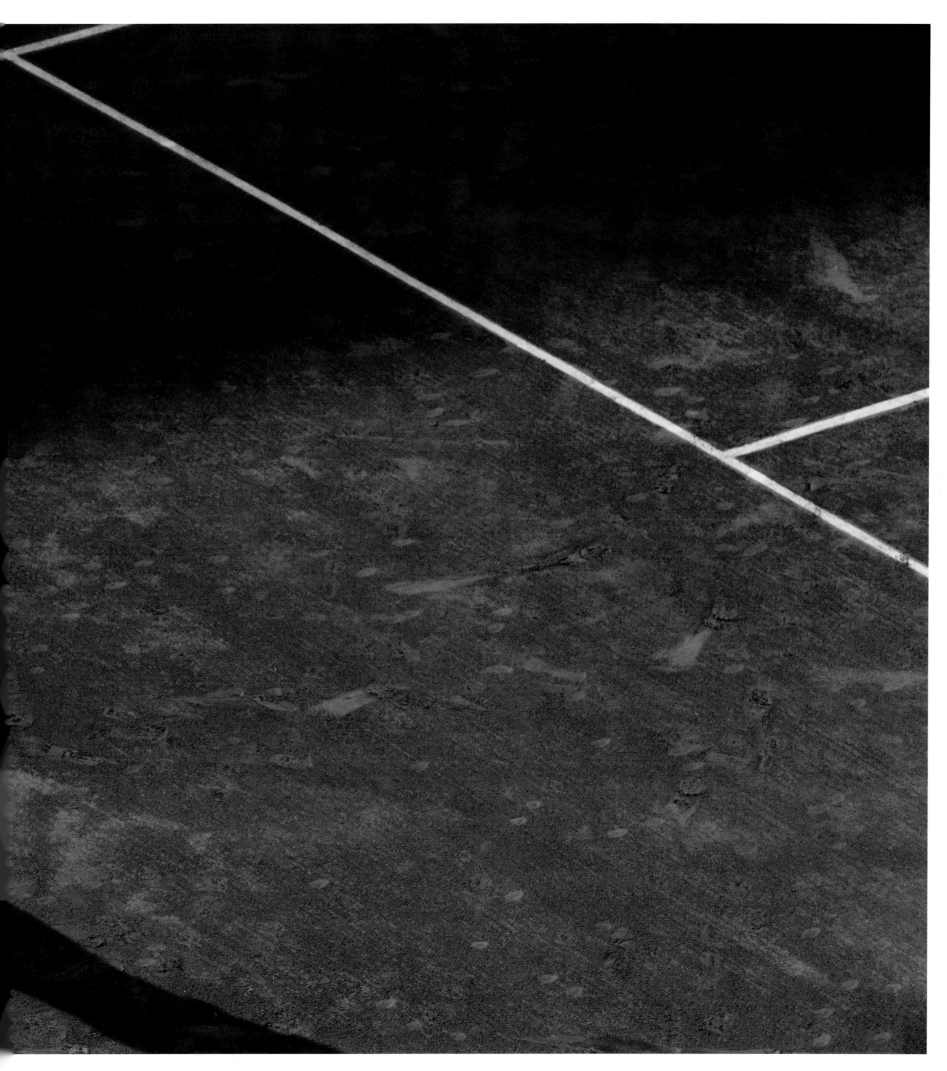

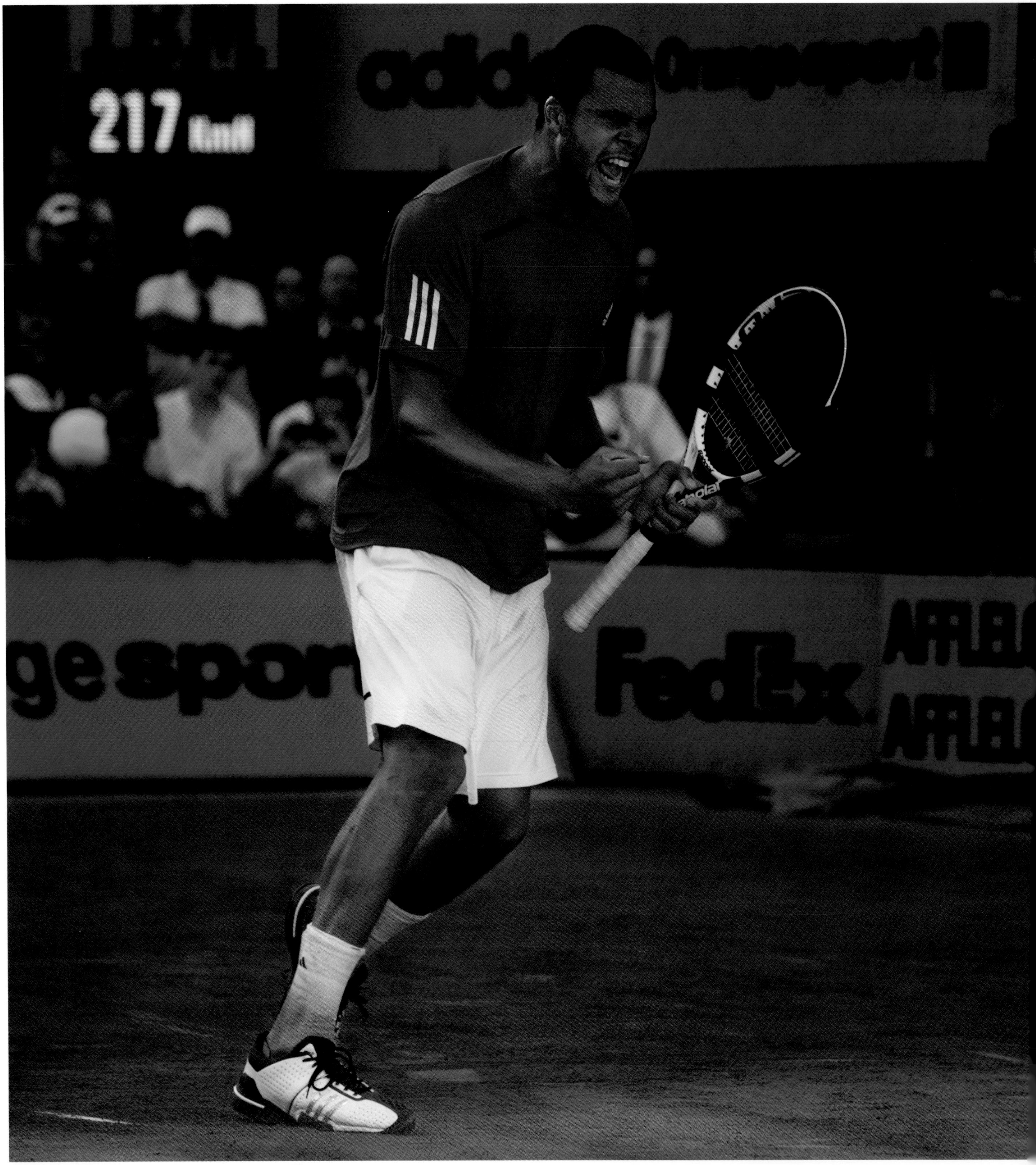
217
FedEx

Man, you cannot be serious!

John McEnroe

It's absolutely essential that you learn to slide and glide on clay at an early age. Jim Courier

Venus Williams came dressed for a cocktail party...and a tennis match broke out. Bill Dwyre

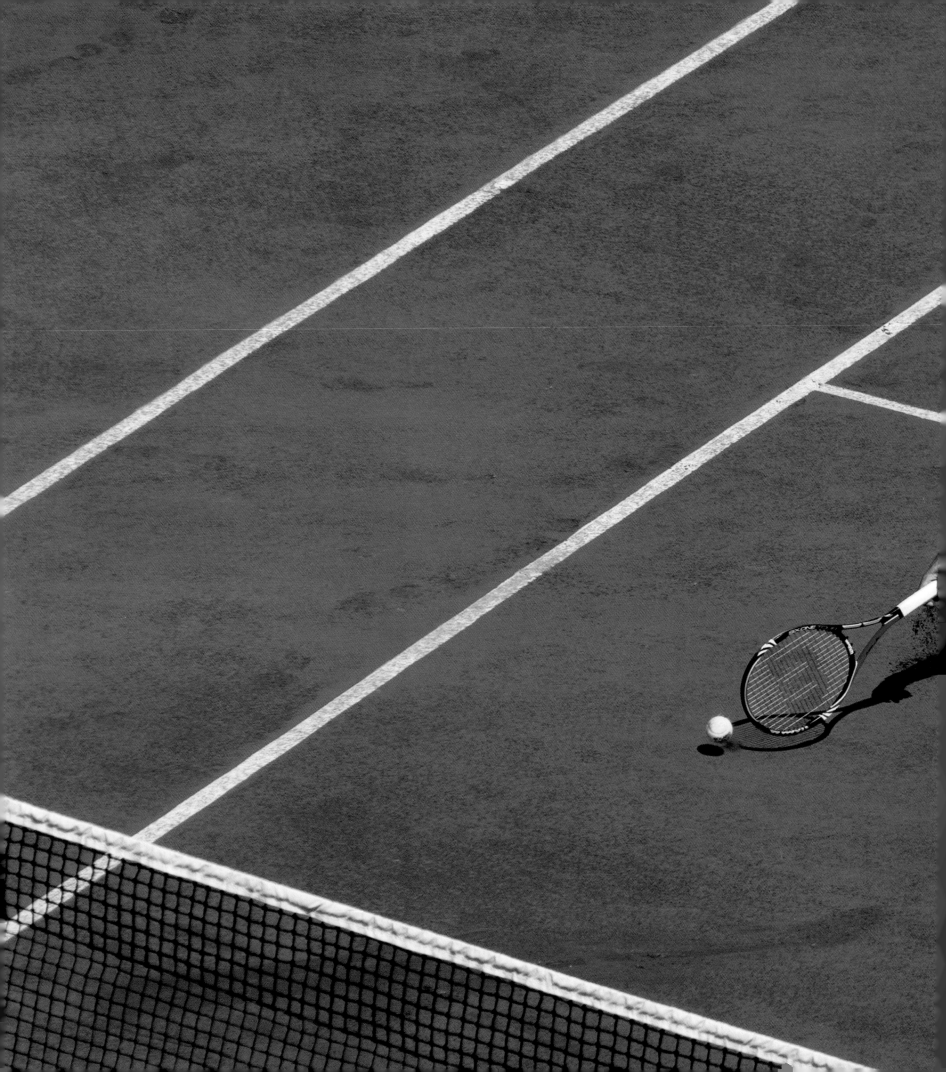

Look, no matter what people say, I never thought my problem was clay.

My problem was Rafa. The guy is unbelievable. Roger Federer

It's a huge pleasure for me to be here in Paris. I won in Paris. I'm very lucky, and I was very fortunate in life to have had the opportunity of experiencing all this at the age of twenty-four. Never in my wildest dream would I have dreamt of such beautiful presents. Rafael Nadal

Wimbledon

The celebrity count is high, and you can
always rely on the Royal Box to confer that
bit of old English snobbery to the event.
But you can also get to be right next to players
on outside courts, and there is something of the
garden party hovering over the lawns.

Mike Powell

The hallowed grounds of Wimbledon…the field of dreams for tennis players…

It's great. It's legendary. James Blake

It's a dream for any player to play opening day on the perfect grass court. Roger Federer

I was fascinated by the gladiators in the arena...the two warriors,

the fight to the death, the crowd rooting for its favorite. Martina Navratilova

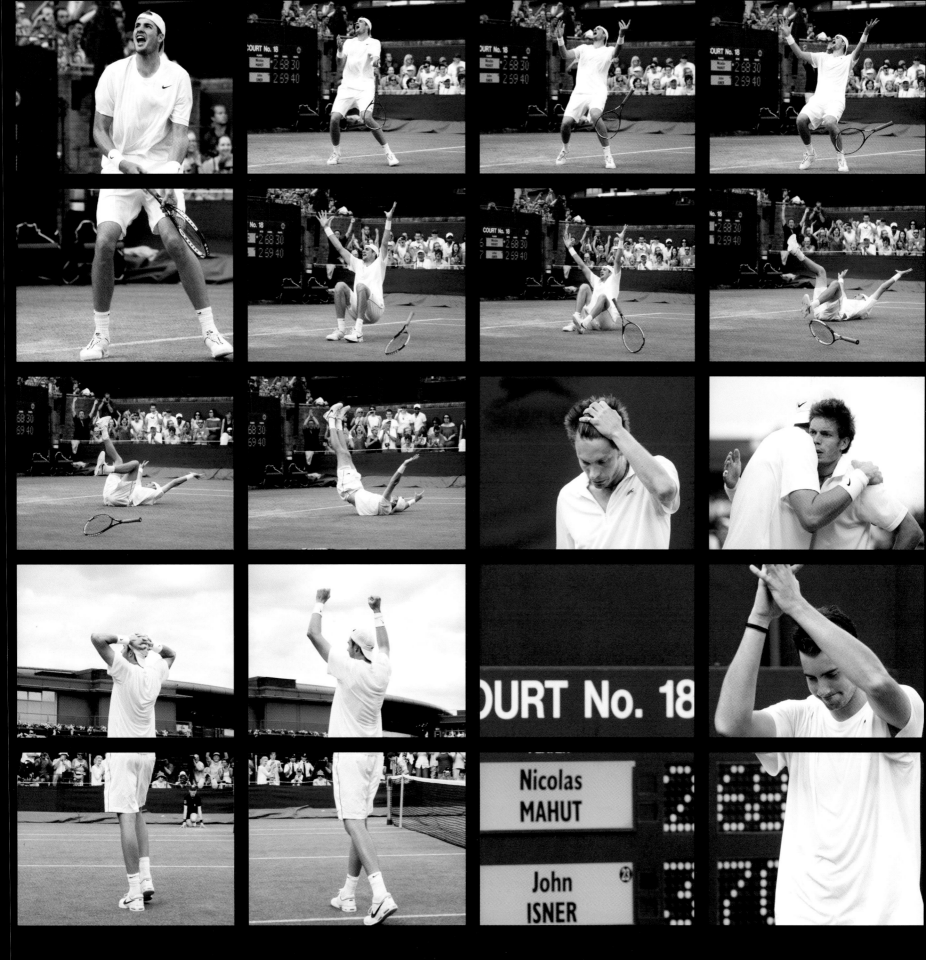

...fighting to the death in front of people who are eating cheese sandwiches,

checking their watches, chatting about the stockmarket. John McEnroe

What is the point of going on court if you don't want to win? Björn Borg

You never expect to beat the best players in the world...but I think that if I play my best tennis, then I have a very good chance of beating all of them. Andy Murray

ndy MURRAY 0
v
afael NADAL • 1
HALLENGES REMAININ
MURRAY
NADAL

New York City

You need to have an audio track for the pictures here—New Yorkers might love the tennis, particularly when it gets tough, but they also love to talk. And if for a moment you can't hear them, it's probably because a plane is passing overhead.

Mike Powell

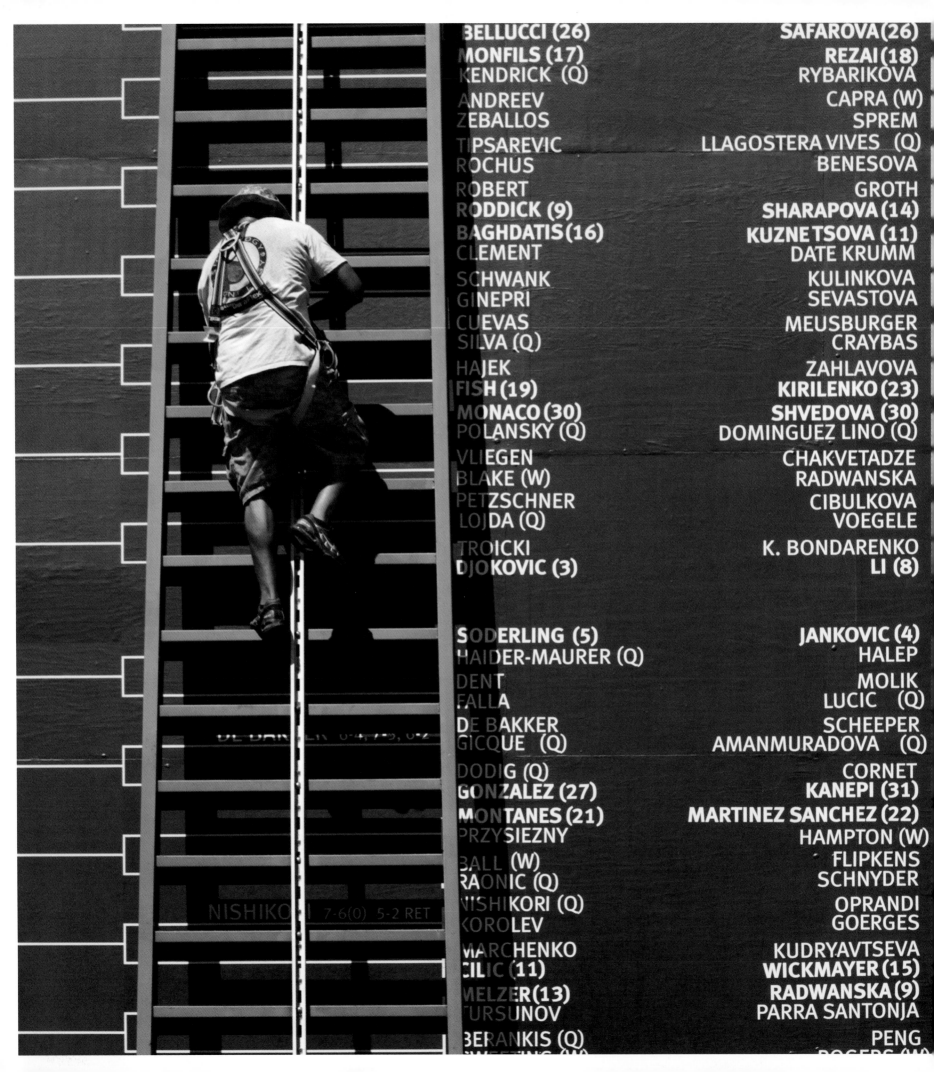

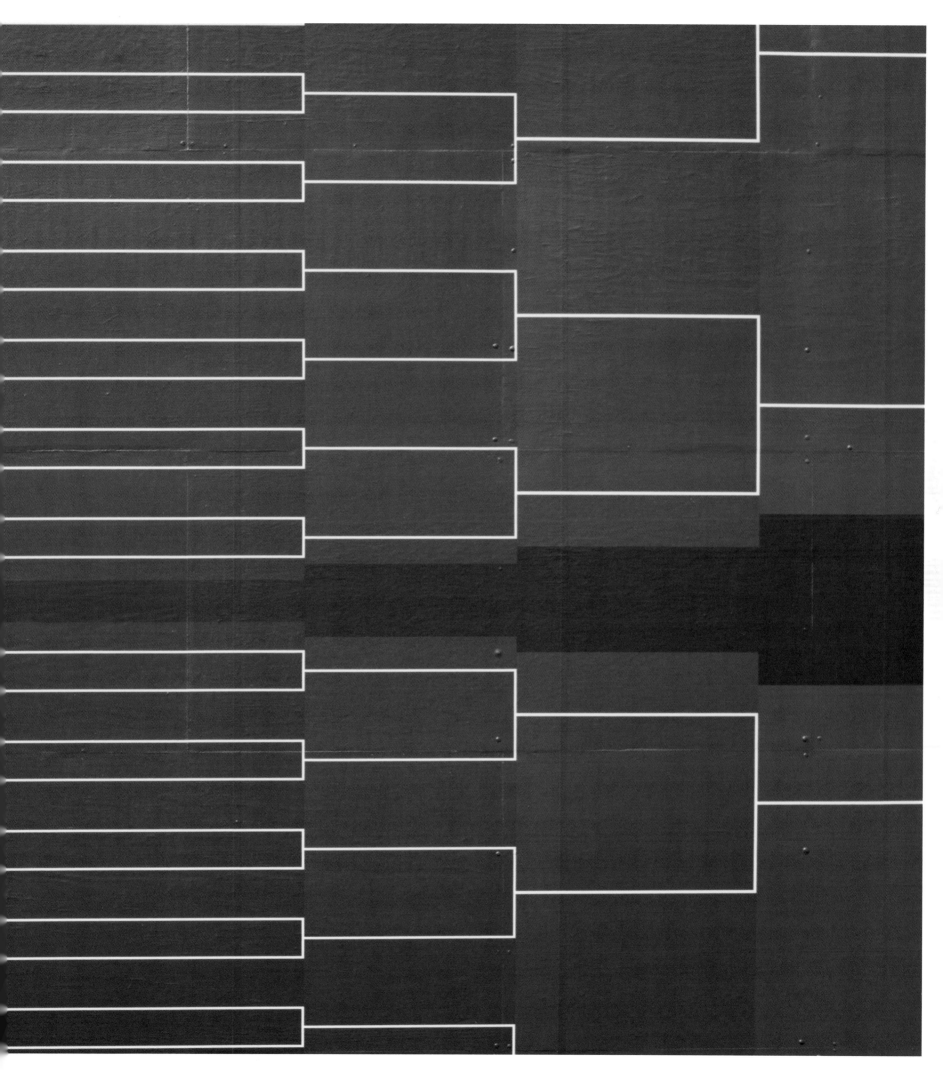

New York is an amazing place for me. It has brought nothing but happiness to my tennis life. Whenever I step on this court [Ashe], it feels like coming home. It is the support from the fans that makes me play better. Kim Clijsters

New Yorkers love it when you spill your guts out there.

Spill your guts at Wimbledon and they make you stop and clean it up. Jimmy Connors

Night tennis is a different world from that of day tennis. The lights, the feel of the court,

the atmosphere: everything moves in a way that it doesn't quite match the way it does under

the sun, like a whole other sport in and of itself. Nicholas McCarvel

I'm a really tough player. I never give up. Doesn't matter what the score is. Caroline Wozniacki

Heineken
TENNIS CHANNEL
Wilson
Panasonic
OLYMPUS
TICKETSNOW
CHASE
Mercedes-Benz

Canon
Mercedes-Benz
Heineken
CITIZEN
IBM
American Express

Next time I face [Nadal], I'm probably going to have to play with two rackets.

That's the only way to beat him when he's in this form. Novak Djokovic

In the first moment [after losing] you're disappointed, you're shocked, you're sad then all of a sudden it overwhelms you. The problem is you

can't go in the locker room and just take it easy and take a cold shower. You can't. You're stuck out there. It's the worst feeling.

Roger Federer

Losing is not my enemy; fear of losing is my enemy. Rafael Nadal

Images

Jacket cover and p. 43: *Rafael Nadal* vs. Andy Murray; case cover: Dustin Brown vs. Andy Murray at the US Open; front endpaper: crowd at the French Open; facing title page: *Dinara Safina* vs. Kumiko Date Krumm at the French Open; pp. 2–3: *Rafael Nadal* vs. Philipp Petzschner at Wimbledon; p. 6: *Venus Williams* vs. Kim Clijsters at the US Open; p. 10: *Richard Gasquet* vs. Andy Murray at the French Open; p. 12: *Rafael Nadal* vs. Lleyton Hewitt at the French Open; p. 15: *Thiemo De Bakker* vs. *Jo-Wilfried Tsonga* at the French Open; p. 16: *Lleyton Hewitt* vs. *Denis Istomin* French Open; p. 18: court surfaces from the Australian Open and the French Open; p. 19: court surfaces from Wimbledon and the US Open

Australian Open
January 2010, Melbourne, Australia

pp. 22–23: *Roger Federer* vs. *Andy Murray*; pp 24–25: signs at the Australian Open; pp. 26–27: *Lleyton Hewitt* vs. *Donald Young*; p. 28: *Gael Monfils*, fans; p. 29: *Rafael Nadal*, fans; p. 30: *Samantha Stosur* vs. Serena Williams; p. 31: *Venus Williams* vs. Na Li; pp. 32–33: *Grega Zemlja* vs. Benjamin Becker; pp. 34–35: *Serena Williams* vs. Urszula Radwanska; p. 36 (left) and p. 37 (left): *Justine Henin* vs. Jie Zheng; p. 36 (right) and p. 37 (right): *Justine Henin* vs. Nadia Petrova; p. 38: *Samantha Stosur* vs. Xinyun Han, (top right) unidentified player, (bottom right) *Gael Monfils* vs. John Isner; p. 39: *Venus Williams, Juan Monaco*, (bottom left) unidentified player; pp. 40–41: *Rafael Nadal* vs. Peter Luczak; pp. 42–43: *Rafael Nadal* vs. Andy Murray; pp. 44–45: *Jie Zheng* vs. Justine Henin; pp. 46–47: *Novak Djokovic* vs. Denis Istomin; pp. 48–49: *Marin Cilic* vs. Andy Murray; p. 50 and p. 51: *Andy Murray* vs. *Roger Federer*; p. 52 and p. 53 (bottom left): *Andy Murray* vs. Marin Cilic, p. 53 (top left and right): *Andy Murray* vs. John Isner; pp. 54–55: *Roger Federer* vs. Igor Andreev; p. 56: *Roger Federer* vs. Jo-Wilfred Tsonga; p. 57: *Roger Federer* vs. Andy Murray; pp. 58–59: *Serena Williams* vs. Urzula Radwanska; pp. 60–61: *Serena Williams* vs. Justine Henin

French Open (Roland Garros)
May–June 2010, Paris, France

pp. 62–63: Roland Garros museum; pp. 64–65: *Rafael Nadal* vs. Horacio Zeballos; pp. 66–67: *Gael Monfils* vs. Fabio Fognini; pp. 68–69: *Fernando Verdasco* vs. *Florent Serra*; pp. 70–71: *Andy Murray*; pp. 72–73: *Fernando Verdasco* vs. Philipp Kohlschreiber; pp. 74–75: *Elena Dementieva* vs. Aleksandra Wozniak; p. 76: *Vania King* in blue top, ball boy, *Caroline Wozniacki* vs. Alexandra Dulgheru; p. 77: *Lleyton Hewitt* vs. *Denis Istomin, Serena Williams'* nails, *Jo-Wilfried Tsonga* in orange top vs. Daniel Brands, *Richard Gasquet* vs. Andy Murray, *Kumiko Date Krumm* in yellow top vs. Dinara Safina, *Maria Kirilenko* in white top vs. Svetlana Kuznetsova,

Victoria Azarenka in pink dress vs. Gisela Dulko; pp. 78–79: *Arnaud Clement* vs. *Alexandr Dolgopolov*; pp. 80–81: *Samantha Stosur* vs. Rossana de los Rios; pp. 82–83: *Jo-Wilfried Tsonga* vs. Daniel Brands; p. 84: *Gianni Mina* vs. Rafael Nadal; p. 85: *Fabio Fognini* vs. Gael Monfils, *Fernando Verdasco* vs. Florent Serra, *Andy Murray* vs. Richard Gasquet; pp. 86–87: *Dinara Safina* vs. Kumiko Date Krumm; pp. 88–89: *Venus Williams* vs. Nadia Petrova; pp. 90–91: *Roger Federer* vs. Peter Luczak; pp. 92–93: *Andy Murray* vs. Richard Gasquet; p. 94–95: *Rossana de los Rios* vs. *Samantha Stosur*; pp. 96–97: *Venus Williams* vs. Patty Schnyder; pp. 98–99: *Serena Williams* vs. Julia Georges; p. 100: *Jelena Jankovic* vs. Kaia Kanepi; p. 101: *Aravane Rezai* vs. Angelique Kerber; pp. 102–103: *Roger Federer* vs. Peter Luczak; pp. 104–105: *Roger Federer* vs. Alejandro Falla; pp. 106–107: *Rafael Nadal* vs. Lleyton Hewitt; pp. 108–109: *Rafael Nadal* vs. Gianni Mina

Wimbledon Championships
June–July 2010, London, England

pp. 110–111: *Roger Federer* vs. *Alejandro Falla*; pp. 112–113: crowd watching center court; pp. 114–115: *Maximo Gonzalez* vs. *Lleyton Hewitt*; pp. 116–119: *Roger Federer* vs. Alejandro Falla; pp. 120–121: *Tsvetana Pironkova* vs. Vera Zvonareva; pp. 122–123: *Sam Querrey* vs. *Sergiy Stakhovsky*; pp. 124–125: the atmosphere at Wimbledon; pp. 126–127: *Andy Roddick* vs. Michael Llodra; pp. 128–129: *Nicolas Mahut* vs. *John Isner*; pp. 130–131: *Mardy Fish* and *Mark Knowles* vs. Philip Marx and Igor Zelenay; pp. 132–133: crowd on Henman Hill, aka *Murray Mound*; p. 134 and p. 135 (bottom left): *Michael Llodra* vs. Andy Roddick; p. 135 (top left): *Andy Murray* vs. Sam Querrey, (right) *Kei Nishikori* vs. Rafael Nadal; p. 136: *Maria Kirilenko* vs. Kim Clijsters; p. 137: *Vera Zvonareva* vs. Tsvetana Pironkova; pp. 138–139: *Novak Djokovic* vs. *Olivier Rochus*; pp. 140–141: *Maria Sharapova* vs. Barbora Zahlavova Strycova; p. 142: *Jo-Wilfried Tsonga* vs Andy Murray; p. 143: *Tomas Berdych* vs. Roger Federer; pp. 144–145: *Jurgen Melzer* and *Philipp Petzschner* vs. Robert Lindstedt and Horia Tecau; p. 146: *Vera Zvonareva* vs. Tsvetana Pironkova; pp. 147–149: *Serena Williams* vs. Vera Zvonareva; pp. 150–151: *Andy Murray* vs. *Jo-Wilfried Tsonga*; p. 152 and p. 153: *Rafael Nadal* vs. *Andy Murray*; pp. 154–155: *Rafael Nadal* vs. Robin Haase; pp. 156–159: *Rafael Nadal* vs. Tomas Berdych

US Open
August–September 2010, New York City, USA

pp. 160–161: US Open practice courts; pp. 162–163: *Maria Sharapova* vs. *Iveta Benesova*; pp. 164–165: scoreboard; p. 166: *Kim Clijsters* vs *Vera Zvonareva*; p. 167 *Kim Clijsters* vs *Venus Williams*; p. 168–169: *Kim Clijsters* vs. Venus Williams; pp. 170–171: *Dinara Safina* vs. Daniela Hantuchova; p. 172: *Venus Williams* vs. Kim Clijsters;

p. 173: *Maria Sharapova* vs. Jarmila Groth; pp. 174–175: *Mikhail Youzhny* vs. Rafael Nadal; pp. 176–177: the atmosphere at the US Open; pp. 178–179: *Jurgen Melzer* vs. Roger Federer; pp. 180–181: *Alize Cornet* vs. *Kaia Kanepi*; pp. 182–183: *Caroline Wozniacki* vs. Vera Zvonareva; pp. 184–185: *Caroline Wozniacki* vs. Maria Sharapova; pp. 186–187: *Novak Djokovic* vs. Rafael Nadal; pp. 188–189: *Novak Djokovic* vs. Viktor Troicki; p. 190 and p. 191 (right): *Roger Federer* vs. Paul-Henri Mathieu; p. 191 (left, top and bottom): *Roger Federer* vs. Andreas Beck; pp. 192–193: *Vera Zvonareva* vs. Kaia Kanepi; pp. 194–195: *Rafael Nadal* vs. Fernando Verdasco; pp. 196–197: *Rafael Nadal* vs. Novak Djokovic; pp. 198–199: *Rafael Nadal*

Back endpaper: crowd at the French Open; jacket back cover: Sebastien Grosjean vs. Marsel Ilhan at the Australian Open

Acknowledgments

Jude, Sean, Emma, and my mum and dad (who banished me to California as a teenager to make my way).

The great athletes who were unknowingly my subjects.

The anvil of Allsport Photography, which helped mold me as a photographer back in the day, including my brother Steve, who tried to talk me out of a life in photography when I was fourteen.

The publisher is grateful for the permission to reproduce the extracts below subject to copyright. Every effort has been made to trace the copyright holders and the publisher apologizes for any unintentional omissions. We would be pleased to hear from any not acknowledged here and undertake to make all reasonable efforts to include the appropriate acknowledgment in any subsequent editions.

From Andy Murray interview, reprinted with permission from Rogers Cub, Toronto, p. 151; From the Australian Open, pp. 29, 50, 54, 191; From "Hurting Before the Open, Venus Is in the Pink Now," copyright © 2010 *Los Angeles Times*, Bill Dwyre, reprinted with permission, p. 96; From *Charging the Net: A History of Blacks in Tennis from Althea Gibson and Arthur Ashe to the Williams Sisters* by Cecil Harris and Larryette Kyle-DeBose, copyright © 2007 Rowman & Littlefield Publishing, reprinted with permission, p. 59; From the French Open, p. 106; From "He Llorado Mucho" by Juan José Mateo, copyright © 2010 *El País*, p. 103; From *Being Myself* by Martina Navratilova with George Vecsey, copyright © 1985 HarperCollins Publishers, p. 126; From "How Power Has Transformed Women's Tennis" by Michael Kimmelman, copyright © 2010 *The New York Times*, p. 35; From *Monica: From Fear to Victory* by Monica Seles with Nancy Ann Richardson, copyright © 1996 HarperCollins Publishers, p. 21; From "The Magic of the US Open at Night" by Nicholas McCarvel, copyright © *The New York Times*, p. 178; From *On Being John McEnroe* by Tim Adams, copyright © 2005 Random House, Inc, p. 135; From "Roland Garros 2010: Roger Federer Still The Man...for Now" by Tim Ruffin, reprinted by permission of Bleacherreport. com, p. 71; From the US Open, pp. 167, 182.

Library of Congress Cataloging-in-Publication Data

Powell, Mike.
A Game to Love : In Celebration of Tennis / Mike Powell.
p. cm.
ISBN 978-1-4197-0001-9 (alk. paper)
1. Tennis—Pictorial works. 2. Tennis—Quotations, maxims, etc. I. Title.
GV996.3.P69 2011
779'.9796342—dc22
2010047268

Produced and originated by PQ Blackwell Limited
116 Symonds Street, Auckland, New Zealand
www.pqblackwell.com
Publisher: Geoff Blackwell
Editor in Chief: Ruth Hobday
Book Design: Cameron Gibb with Victoria Skinner

ABRAMS
THE ART OF BOOKS SINCE 1949
115 West 18th Street
New York, NY 10011
www.abramsbooks.com